GW00675302

FINANCIAL

FREEDOM

Doing Nothing is an Option

EDMUND H. MOORE, PhD

Lift Bridge Publishing

Disclaimer Statement:

This publication contains the opinions and ideas of the author based on life experiences. It is intended to provide helpful and useful information on the topics covered. It is sold with the intent that the author and publisher are not engaged in providing professional services through this book. Throughout this book, the author advises the reader or listener to seek professional advice from a competent professional.

The author and publisher specifically disclaim any responsibility for any liability, loss or risk, personal or otherwise, which is incurred as a consequence, directly or indirectly, of the use and application of this books contents.

Copyright

All rights reserved. No part of this publication may be used either in print or electronic form without the written consent of ---- Publishing. This book is published in the United States (U.S.) by Lift Bridge Publishing.

For information regarding personal appearances, interviews please contact O-Media Group.

Cover Photograph by:

Edited by: Ms. Carla M. Dean,
U Can Mark My Word

ISBN
9798885675789

FINANCIAL

FREEDOM

Doing Nothing is an Option

DEDICATION

I dedicate this book to my late best friend, Richard R. Napier Sr.—a Vietnam veteran who was to be my co-author on this book before his untimely death. He was a modern-day scholar, Renaissance man, and griot.

And to my beautiful daughters, Mackenzie and Madison, who give me the honor of being their father.

TABLE OF CONTENTS

ACKNOWLEDGMENTS

The creation of this book has been a long time coming. Many folks have asked me for financial guidance over the past few decades based on their perception of what I accomplished in the setup of my finances—investments, savings, major purchases, education, insurance, and other items. I have made many presentations on this topic.

I thank my children, Mackenzie and Madison, for supporting me during several major life transitions.

I acknowledge the late Richard R. Napier Sr., who was to be my co-author on this book. Although he was unable to provide any written content, we had many lively discussions regarding this book writing project. I thank his family for sharing him with me and others.

Thanks to James Martin and Dr. Karen Bright for filling the breach. Brother Martin disliked the title tagline, "Doing Nothing is an Option." He advocated that "one must start with the end in mind and have a plan to be successful."

I thank my brother, niece, and family, who are always in my corner and encouraging me. Thanks to my publicist Olivia Almagro, who continues to push me to write and do interviews, even though I have a full-time job. And thanks to my business partners, publisher, and editors.

I thank my friends from high school, undergraduate college (FAMU), and the various graduate schools (M.I.T., UF, Antioch McGregor) for their encouragement.

And I truly thank my church family, especially the Courage to Change Sunday School class members of the Omega Baptist Church in Dayton, Ohio. I kept getting the same command: "You got to write that book." And write that book I did. To all, thank you!

INTRODUCTION

Life is a contact sport defined by a series of our daily choices. Every day, I am the one who decides what to wear, what to eat, and what to do. As a person who has gone through many strategic planning exercises, one option always on the table is: Do nothing. *Dolce far niente*—as the Italian idiom goes. The sweetness of doing nothing.

However, if this nothingness extends the length of your work ethic and productivity scale, sweet eventually turns bitter. Despite this option being contrary to what one should do, it is the default option many have chosen. Strategic planning gives you the luxury of knowing where you are going and how you plan to get there. The best practice is to start with the end in mind.

I will be using many analogies, examples, and personal life experiences to clearly pave the road to achieving financial freedom. I intend to provide a route of many steps to prepare your family and yourself to achieve financial freedom. Please note that this process will not be all-encompassing, as you will need to think for yourself, seek help, and educate your family and yourself during your lifetime. If you have achieved most of what I present in this book, congratulations. Teach others what you have achieved.

We all start at different stages of life. We all come into the world naked. Some—like the heirs of Bill Gates (Microsoft), Sam Walton (Wal-Mart), and Rihanna—may be worth millions of dollars when they are born. I was worth whatever my parents had accumulated on my behalf to share with me. Others are born into families with no appreciable assets and may even inherit debts. In the end, even if you are blessed to inherit wealth, you will blow the much if you can't handle the little. Think of lottery winners who go from overnight wealth to utter ruin in a matter of years.

Our charge to you is as follows: Avoid the default route of "doing nothing." Stop procrastinating, start with the end in mind, set goals, and GET STARTED on the journey to achieving FINANCIAL FREEDOM.

CHAPTER 1

FINANCIAL FREEDOM TO GENERATIONAL WEALTH

The Bottom Line Upfront (BLUF)

Financial Freedom to Generational Wealth

- Generational Wealth
- Financial Freedom
- The "Pulled Myself Up by the Bootstrap" Myth

L et's start by defining two terms: generational wealth and financial freedom—the precursor to generational wealth.

Generational wealth is simply the ability to provide financially for your children and your children's children. An incomplete listing of this wealth can consist of cash, real estate, securities, royalties, or family business ownership. A Bible verse that touches on this is Proverbs 13:22 (NKJV): *A good man leaves an inheritance to his children's children.* The second half of that verse says, *But the wealth of the sinner is stored up for the righteous.* Thank goodness for that storehouse.

I view myself as a third-generational wealth person. Why a third generation? I consider the first generation as my grandfather, Lee Moore Sr., and my father's household of George R. Moore Sr. as the second generation. My household, Edmund H. Moore, is the third generation. Our family was blessed thanks to my grandfather, who left 40 acres of land to his 12 children in Eufaula, Alabama. They sold that property and divided up the proceeds amongst themselves. Even before that distribution, my father and mother built homes, worked, saved, and invested.

For the most part, my parents were public school educators who provided my brother and me with a college education. After their death, they left behind property, financial proceeds, and assets. That is a personal example of generational wealth transfer. Proverbs 10:22 (NIV): *The blessing of the Lord brings wealth, without painful toil for it.*

In most cases, one must achieve financial freedom in order to be in a position to transfer generational wealth. An exception could be a large life insurance policy allowing for the generational wealth opportunity.

I define **financial freedom** as the ability to pay off my family's living expenses in perpetuity (a fancy word for forever) without touching the principal (core financial assets). That is true financial freedom. There is an old Supreme Court Justice Potter Stewart saying about obscenity: 'I know it when I see it.' Likewise, one can come up with many attributes of what financial freedom looks like. For example, not having to worry about going to the doctor, not having to stress about making a major household purchase, being able to hire others to do one's household work like lawn maintenance and household cleaning, and lastly, being able to go on vacations.

The benefits of generational wealth allow the following generations to achieve their goals and dreams more easily without the burden of debt. They get the chance to live in better neighborhoods with access to better education, nutrition, safety, clean environments, and opportunities. However, future success is not guaranteed.

The negative of not benefiting from generational wealth is that one has to start from the ground floor to build up. A possible analogy of both situations: Picture two individuals competing in a 100-meter race—one is posed at the start line with a 50-pound backpack tied to his back, whereas the competitor is at the 50-meter mark with no backpack weighing him down. I'm assuming you can surmise which one is bestowed with the upper hand of generational wealth.

In conclusion, there is no such thing as **I pulled myself up by my bootstraps**. Why? We all rely on others in this life. We did not build the physical infrastructure, legal structures, intellectual property, and so forth that allow one to succeed. We all reside in a community, and no one can elevate themselves without outside assistance.

CHAPTER 2

WHAT DO YOU ACTUALLY OWN AND INVENTORY

BLUF—What You Actually Own

◆ Financial Assets
◆ Non-Financial Assets
◆ Do a Self-Inventory of Your Assets
◆ Do a Self-Inventory of Your Family Assets

What do you actually own? And how do you catalog what you own? The types of ownership categories come down to financial and non-financial assets.

Financial assets include savings, checking, money market accounts, and certificates of deposit (CDs) for short-term usage. As one looks at holding funds for over a year, say 18 months or longer, one may consider stocks (known as equities), bonds, and mutual funds. It is a "best practice" for most people to avoid day trading equities (stocks).

Newer asset classes include blockchain-related ones, such as Non-Fungible Tokens (NFTs) and Crypto assets like Bitcoin, Coinbase, Ethereum, and many others. There are many longer-term assets, such as 401(k), 403 (b), 457(b), Traditional Individual Retirement Accounts (IRAs), ROTH IRAs, and Simplified Employee Pension (SEP).

Some specialized tax-advantaged accounts include Health Saving Accounts (HSA), Educational Savings Accounts (ESA), College Education 529 Plans, and others.

Non-financial investments may include what you wear, where you live, your transportation means, and other associated items. Tangible property such as homes, jewelry, artwork, collectibles, antiques, boats, cars, land, royalties, and other items are also considered non-financial assets.

EXERCISE: Using a sheet of paper or an electronic spreadsheet, take inventory of what you own. Then, do the same for and with your family. By the way, if you have a car with money still owed on the loan, even if the amount is only $10, that vehicle is not yours. Pay it off. It is a great practice to pay off all items within your agreement to ensure full ownership of the item.

When I look at what I own, I do the following. First, I look at what I own against all my debts. Outright, I own a home and jointly own a piece of property (land). I have a car, furniture, appliances, clothes, electronics, artwork, shoes, beds, and other household items. Next, I look at other financial assets: paid-up insurance, retirement accounts, private investments, partnerships, bank and credit union accounts, and other related investments.

Oh, how blessed I am! Now it's your turn to count your blessings and take inventory of what you actually own.

CHAPTER 3

WHAT DO YOU OWE

BLUF—What You Owe

- ◆ Short-Term Debt
- ◆ Medium-Term Debt
- ◆ Long-Term Debt
- ◆ Family Debt

Ask yourself **what you owe.** What are your debts? Include your mortgage if you have one. Your debt can be divided into three categories: short-term, intermediate-term or medium-term, and long-term. Let's take a look at my personal debts. I have a Home Equity Line of Credit (HELOC) Loan that may be referred to as a second mortgage on my home, a car loan, a Thrift Savings Plan (TSP), a loan from my 401(k) equivalent, and a personal loan from a family member. That's it.

Do you have **short-term debts**? Examples of short-term debts are monthly credit card payments, monthly household expenses, and any debt agreements you are scheduled to pay in full within a year. (For example, a computer purchased that you will pay off within a year). An accountant would break them into sterile categories, such as accounts payable, taxes due, short-term loans, and wages due to employees.

Intermediate-term or medium-term debts may include debts that cover 2 to 10 years. These could consist of payment arrangements for cars, boats, furniture, and property improvements. Surprisingly, some car payments now extend out 7 to 10 years.

Long-term debts may include home mortgages lasting from 10 to 30 years. Some may even be 40 to 50 years in length. The purchasing of property can fall into this timeframe, as well. Mortgage rates can be fixed or adjustable; it is a "best practice" to be extremely careful with variable rates.

Is there such a thing as **family debt**? If you are a married couple, debts incurred during the marriage are not necessarily individual debts (e.g., credit cards and other purchases). They belong to the married couple, regardless of who incurred the debt. A person's education loan would not be considered a family debt unless both parties signed off upon the loan. Depending on how one files their taxes, that decision may affect future debt ownership. That is why it is good for both individuals and married couples to seek guidance from a tax practitioner, attorney, or Certified Public Accountant (CPA) on individual and family debt matters.

Note: Please remember that you do not own an asset unless it is fully paid off based on the terms of the agreement. Make a list of everything you owe (your debts). Then pay off your debts as soon as possible to avoid paying interest or defaulting.

CHAPTER 4

NET WORTH

BLUF—Your Net Worth

- ◆ What is Your Net Worth
- ◆ The Wealth Gap (U.S.)
- ◆ Financial Record Retention

After you have done your self-inventory of what you own and owe, you have placed a stake in the ground for you and your family to start adding to or creating generational wealth. However, before you start your plan, it is crucial to know your net worth. And please realize that not everyone will become financially rich in their generation—John 12:8 (NIV) "You will always have the poor among you…" There will also be the poor in spirit. The upside is that if you manage to achieve generational wealth, you are in a position to alleviate your family's stress and poverty.

Calculating your **net worth** is an easy and essential financial exercise. The mathematical equation is:

$$\text{Net Worth} =$$
$$\text{Assets (Financial + Non-financial)} - \text{All Outstanding Liabilities}$$

or

$$\text{Net Worth (NW)} = \text{Assets (A)} - \text{Debts (D)}$$

Many people own automobiles, homes, furnishings, and other household items. Additionally, they possess financial assets saved in banks, credit unions, retirement accounts, brokerage and mutual fund investments, and private investments not held in formal accounts, such as rental properties, insurance products, and 529 college savings plans. Please note that private investments are mostly illiquid, which means one may be unable to convert them to cash quickly. Brokerage, bank, and credit union accounts are liquid; therefore, one may quickly access their cash. Know the difference between **liquid and illiquid assets**.

My debts include a loan against my Thrift Savings Plan (TSP), and a Home Equity Line of Credit loan against my home.

My net worth is determined by adding up my assets and then subtracting the total of my debts from my assets. If that number is positive, I have a positive net worth. If that number is negative, then I am in debt. The higher your net worth number, the better your finances. This is a time for aspirational thinking about wealth.

There is a **significant wealth gap in the U.S.** between Black, Latino, Hispanic, Asian, Native Americans, and whites. According to https://www.statista.com, the top ten percent in the U.S. as of Q1 of 2021 held 69.8% of the total U.S. net worth (the value of all assets a person has minus their liabilities). The top one percent held about half of that wealth at 32.1%, while the next nine percent held about another half at 37.7%. That left 30.2% for the remaining ninety percent.

I asked my brother once, "What do you think about wealth, real wealth?"

He responded, "Are you talking Negro wealth or *true* wealth?"

"What is the difference?"

"A Negro thinks they're rich with $100,000 to $200,000. True wealth is having at least $8 million in net worth."

Others like my brother equate real wealth to an even higher number, such as $50 to $75 million. So, be aspirational. Know your personal number that makes you comfortable enough to stop working and retire—and hopefully transfer generational wealth.

What records should a family maintain (i.e., **financial record retention**)? Maintain the contact information (names, addresses, telephone numbers, and email addresses) for your employer (e.g., supervisor), financial advisors, tax preparer or accountant, insurance agents, medical physicians, and attorneys (trust, will, etc.). This is covered in more detail in this book's *Documenting Your Life Information* section.

For the documents that you retain, you need to maintain account numbers, relevant passwords, and access for your family in case you become disabled or even pass.

The documents you should maintain include:
- Bank accounts
- Brokerage accounts (taxable and retirement)
- 401(k), TSP, and others
- Bonds
- Private equity contracts
- Personal loan agreements
- Home mortgage or ownership paperwork
- Auto loan or ownership paperwork
- Insurance policies

- ◆ Social Security or other annuity benefit records
- ◆ Tax records for five years (indefinitely for homes)
- ◆ Estate planning documents (trusts, wills, etc.)
- ◆ Recurring bills and outstanding debts

Be sure to retain maintenance and improvement records for homes and other properties, such as vehicles.

CHAPTER 5

THREE PURPOSES OF MONEY

BLUF—Three Purposes for Money
♦ Spend Money
♦ Save/Invest Money
♦ Give Money Away

One can do three things with money: **spend it, save/invest it,** or **give it away** (as in a charitable donation). I can think of a fourth purpose—burning it for heat if you have too much.

Story from my late friend Richard R. Napier, Sr.:

When we were in school, I noticed that Edmund would buy a large bag of potato chips. He would purchase sandwich bags and place an equal amount of chips into each bag. For that day, he would not eat more than was in that bag. That showed me his discipline.

Like that story, we all must be disciplined to save our money for future needs. By the way, my grandfather, Lee Moore Sr., pretended to have a smoking habit to save money. He put aside money on a regular basis to purchase these imaginary cigarettes. That is how he saved up to get the 40 acres of land.

Some folks advocate that you should save a third, spend a third, and give away a third of your earnings. Others have advocated that you give the first 10% of your income to God as a tithe to your church, spend no more than 35% on housing, put 15% into savings, and live off the remaining 40%. Others even advance a 10:10:80 rule of giving away 10% of your income, saving 10%, and living off 80%. Whatever philosophy you adopt, build a family culture (a life-long process) of giving, saving, and living within your means.

At this stage of my life, I save/invest at least 10% of my income, donate at least 11% to charitable causes, and live off the rest. Proverbs 3:9-10 (NIV): *Honor the Lord with your wealth, with the first fruits of all your crops; then your barns will be filled to overflowing, and your vats will brim over with new wine.* Due to the Lord's grace, I now have a more flexible use for money and invest in uplifting financial and charitable opportunities when they present themselves.

CHAPTER 6

SPIRITUAL AND CULTURAL PURPOSE FOR MONEY

BLUF—The Purposes for Money

- ♦ To Serve the Lord's Purpose
- ♦ To Take Care of Family
- ♦ To Invest in Opportunities
- ♦ To Be Charitable

The purpose of money is not to become rich. For believers, it is a source from your Creator to build up the Kingdom of God and your community. Deuteronomy 8:18 (NIV): *But remember the Lord your God, for it is he who gives you the ability to produce wealth, and so confirms his covenant, which he swore to your ancestors, as it is today.* God requires that we give Him a portion of His blessings back **to serve His purpose.**

We are to build a culture of spiritual finances within ourselves and our families. To **take care of family**, keep this topic of the purpose for money family focused. There must be a life-long education and practice process to change the family culture. The Bible states that as a man (or woman) thinks, so is he (or she). Proverbs 21:2 (NIV): *A person may think their own ways are right, but the Lord weighs the heart.* We should adopt the mindset that prosperity is from God versus man.

Always utilize **family** to practice life-long learning about finances. Discuss finances. Add a certain topic to the schedule and revisit it periodically. Think routine. Be sure to **invest in financial opportunities** as good stewards of your finances. Also, expose the family to financial practitioners (bankers, insurance agents, investment advisors, etc.).

Story:

My late friend Richard R. Napier Sr. sponsored and mentored High School International Science Fair Grand Award Winners in 1993 and 1994. The local newspaper recognized the runner-up honoree over the winner with the excuse that they had worked hard. In his wry response, Richard stated that he relieved himself the first thing every morning for many years, and no one ever recognized him for that.

I definitely recommend monitoring your finances on a remote-control schedule like that, yet not as regularly. Luke 16:11 (NIV): *So if you have not been trustworthy in handling worldly wealth, who will trust you with true riches?*

If one is living within their means, it means they have enough money to cover all expenses and hopefully save some money. To live within our means, we must be content with our blessings. Of course, that doesn't imply that we shouldn't have larger-than-life aspirations and constantly seek to grow. However, we should do so within a spiritual framework of gratitude and be content with God's provisions. Ecclesiastes 5:19 (NIV) says: *Moreover, when God gives someone wealth and possessions, and the ability to enjoy them, to accept their lot and be happy in their toil—this is a gift of God.* My late dad, George R. Moore, Sr., said, "To be happy, do not want so much."

Be **charitable** with your resources. Jesus clearly said that the poor would be with us always. Deuteronomy 15:11 (NIV): *There will always be poor people in the land. Therefore I command you to be openhanded toward your fellow Israelites who are poor and needy in your land.*

If you are a Christian believer, view all of your money and possessions as belonging to the Lord. Proverbs 3:27 (NIV): *Do not withhold good from those to whom it is due, when it is in your power to act.* It is a blessing for us to be able to give back to God and man for his manifold blessings.

Finally, the wicked and the righteous treat financial resources differently. Psalms 37:21 (NIV): *The wicked borrow and do not repay, but the righteous give generously.* There is a spiritual reason for doing what is right in this physical realm where we live. And remember whom wealth belongs to. Haggai 2:8 (NIV) says: *'The silver is mine and the gold is mine,' declares the Lord Almighty.*

CHAPTER 7

THE DIRTY B-WORD

BLUF—Budgets are Important

- Budgets Define Your Priorities
- Example Budget (for illustration purposes only)
- Budget Allocations (examples)

What is a budget? The dirty B-word is budget. A **budget** is simply a method to allocate or direct your income to fund your priorities. The three basic human needs are food, safety, and shelter—then all else. We all desire to belong and have freedom (autonomy), power, and fun.

For example, I am a single person with a monthly income of $3,000 with a nominal budget of ten items: shelter, transportation, food, clothing, charitable, entertainment, insurance, savings, a rainy-day fund, and a category for other unexpected expenses. Thus, my allocation may be as follows (this is just a raw example):

- ◆ Shelter $900
- ◆ Transportation $350
- ◆ **Savings** $325
- ◆ **Charitable** $300
- ◆ Food $275
- ◆ Insurance $200
- ◆ Other $200
- ◆ Clothing $150
- ◆ Entertainment $150
- ◆ Rainy Day Fund $150

The main thing with this **budget illustration** is to show that every dollar has a home. The other, or miscellaneous, line of the budget covers the unanticipated items that may not fit under one of the above categories. When one has children, the budget expands to include childcare expenses. The charitable line is covered by Malachi 3:10 (NIV): *"Bring the whole tithe into the storehouse, that there may be food in my house. Test me in this," says the Lord Almighty, "and see if I will not throw open the floodgates of heaven and pour out so much blessing that there will not be room enough to store it."*

Earlier, we discussed several types of **budget allocations**. One was to give your first 10% to God as a tithe to your church, spend no more than 35% of your income on housing, save 15%, and live off the remaining 40%. There is no right answer here, but I suggest saving at least 10% of your income to invest in your retirement and additional funds for other reasons. Not everyone believes in God, and not all those who believe in Him tithe a portion of their income. If you are one of those who do not, be sure to be charitable with your income in other ways.

Best Practice:

One of the best ways to develop your budget is to track your expenses for three months. Do it on a spreadsheet with an app like Mint or Wallet; the old-school method of pen and paper works just as well. Extend this practice to six months. That gives you a reliable structure of what you spend over six months, capturing all of your annual expenses to budget.

Make changes to your budget as new expense categories arise. For example, as one approaches middle age, they may purchase Long-Term Care (LTC) insurance.

To close, when tracking expenses, keeping good records is a must. Proverbs 21:5 (NIV): *The plans of the diligent lead to profit as surely as haste leads to poverty.*

The major thing about budgets is that you set up one and adhere to it. Based on your budget allocations, you should know the condition of your estate or holdings. Proverbs 27:23-24 (NIV): *Be sure you know the condition of your flocks, give careful attention to your herds; for riches do not endure forever, and a crown is not secure for all generations.*

CHAPTER 8

EMERGENCY/RAINY DAY FUNDS

BLUF—Emergency Funds

- ◆ Establish an Emergency Fund
- ◆ Use Cash or Cash Equivalents
- ◆ Credit Options (last option)
- ◆ Avoid High-Interest Payday Loans

Have you ever experienced an emergency or rainy day without access to adequate funds to solve the situation? The **emergency fund** is also referred to as a rainy day fund since when it rains, one needs protection in the form of an umbrella or rain gear. Based on your stage in life, your emergency fund should cover six months to a year of expenses. The Bible informs us that we are to spend wisely and set aside (encumber) funds, as found in Proverbs 23:5 (NIV): *Cast but a glance at riches, and they are gone, for they will surely sprout wings and fly off to the sky like an eagle.*

This financial source should be **cash or cash equivalents**. Bank accounts or money in investment accounts that are accessible without incurring any fees qualify as this fund source. Cryptocurrencies like Bitcoin may not qualify as liquid assets. Then again, I may not be an appropriate judge of that, given that my knowledge in the area of cryptocurrency is lacking.

A Home Equity Line of Credit (HELOC), credit cards, bank loans, or loans of any form (payday) are not real rainy day funds. Various **credit options** that include **payday loans** are a worse option and a crutch to temporarily get you through a situation that potentially leaves you with even more debt.

It was publicly reported a few years ago that a family member required $500 to get out of a jam, but their extended family lacked the means to assist. The family member that needed the funds subsequently died. This is the classic situation of an individual not having a rainy day fund to assist a family member in need. (Of course, it's a different scenario—and perhaps worse—if the individual refrained from helping out for selfish reasons). According to 1 Timothy 5:8 (NIV): *Anyone who does not provide for their relatives, and especially for their own household, has denied the faith and is worse than an unbeliever.*

Recent statistics by Bankrate.com reveal that only 4 in 10 Americans have enough savings to cover an unplanned (emergency) expense of $1,000. Do not place yourself in that situation that could easily be resolved by saving $10, $25, $50, or $100 per month until you reach your goal.

CHAPTER 9

DEBT

BLUF—Types of Debt

♦ Bad Types of Debt
♦ Good Types of Debt
♦ Budget Allocations

Some sources say there are no good forms of debt. In other words, they believe one must save up and pay for everything with cash. It is a blessing to be in that situation; however, not all of us have that luxury.

Typically, **bad debts** are private student loans, predatory loans, unpaid credit card bills, and high-interest borrowing for any items, products, or services. You may consider personal loans to friends or relatives and not paying your taxes in a timely manner to be other forms of bad debt.

Good debts are typically defined as federal-backed school loans (if and only if your degree leads to employment that can reasonably pay off the loans or if there is a loan forgiveness program), home or property mortgages, and other real asset loans that can be paid off over a reasonable period of time.

For the bulk majority of us, we do not live in a world where we have the cash to pay off everything. If we need a replacement car or a place to live, that may be a problem. Let us assume we have $500 to our name and are blessed to have a source of income (a job or self-employed). If the deposit on a living space is $500, what do we do? That is the situation for many who do not have the $500. An old piece of advice would have been to move in with others or with your parents. That was sound advice before the COVID pandemic, yet it may not be a viable option in a pandemic. Circumstances and strategies change.

The Bible gives us a strategy for how we are to prepare to pay our bills. 1 Corinthians 16:2 (NIV): *On the first day of every week, each one of you should set aside a sum of money in keeping with your income, saving it up, so that when I come no collections will have to be made.*

What more does the Bible say about debt? The Bible covers a lot of territory about finances. For example, debt makes you a slave to the lender in Proverbs 22:7 (NIV): *The rich rule over the poor, and the borrower is slave to the lender.* In conclusion, name one sane person who grows up desiring to be a slave.

CHAPTER 10

DEBT PAYOFF STRATEGIES

BLUF—Debt Payoff Strategies

- ♦ Pay the Highest Interest Debts First
- ♦ Pay the Lowest Loan Amount First
- ♦ Pay your Taxes First (esp. the IRS)
- ♦ Establish Credit by Paying Bills on Time

Many people are plagued by debt. The stress from debt can be so heavy that it affects a person mentally and physically. Therefore, it is essential to one's health to focus on eliminating their debt. A great principle is to **pay off the highest interest debts first**.

Example #1 — A person has two loans. The loans are $10,000 each——one has a 15% interest rate and the other a 5% interest rate. This is straightforward. Pay the minimum each month on the 5% loan and use any additional cash to pay off the highest interest rate loan first. The upside to this approach is paying less interest over the time of both loans. A "best practice" is to see if the higher interest loan—or any loan—can be reduced to a lower interest rate.

Example #2 — A person has two loans. One has a 15% interest rate and the other a 5% interest rate. The loan with the higher interest rate is $10,000, and the loan with the lower interest rate is $600. Focus on **paying off the lowest loan** of $600 to eliminate that debt. The advantage here is that you have eliminated a loan (and it feels good). In parallel, see if you can refinance the remaining high-interest loan to a lower rate.

Example #3 — A person has a $5,000 tax debt with the Internal Revenue Service (IRS) and a $10,000 car loan with a 15% interest rate. Be sure to **pay off the IRS debt first** while maintaining the payments on your car loan. The intent here is to eliminate the risk of default with the IRS and the resultant penalties that may include imprisonment.

Personal Stories:

While a graduate student at the University of Florida, I was living off part-time jobs and a meager graduate fellowship of about $6,000 per year (later to be replaced with a $10,000 per year graduate fellowship). I moved into a trailer park on the recommendation of Richard Napier, Sr. to cut down on rent. I believe an apartment was about $300-$450 per month. My monthly trailer park fee was $120, which included $20 to purchase the trailer over three years and a trailer park lot rent of $100. I was on a three-year plan to buy the trailer at $20 each month for a total of $720. I sold that 1973 trailer for $1,000 when I graduated.

Later in graduate school at the University of Florida, I went to purchase a new car after getting a job with the Air Force. My credit union told me that I did not have any credit. Why? I had no credit because I had not established credit with credit cards or through major purchases that I made regular payments for over a period of time. However, with my Air Force salary, I obtained a simple loan to pay off my car over five years and even started making extra monthly payments. So what did the credit union do? They stopped sending the monthly bills for my payments. The last thing they wanted was for me to pay off the loan early because they would make less money off my purchase since I wouldn't be paying as much interest.

However, I noticed that the principal on my car loan was not going down even with the additional payments. I fixed that issue by visiting the credit union and requesting that the extra payments be applied directly towards the loan's principal, and I paid off the car in one year. The moral of the story is to watch your payment statements very closely for shenanigans.

I was able to pay off my debts by purchasing my needs versus my wants. I patiently paid off the debt on the trailer over 36 months to own it outright, and I impatiently paid off my car four years ahead of the loan agreement, which **established my credit**.

My late friend, Richard Napier, Sr., was invested in a payday loan service in the 1990s with a helpful component. First, they undercharged all of the local payday loan providers. (For example, if the competitor charged 10%, they charged 7%). They also had an in-house tax preparer who helped the clients get on a budget to eliminate the need for payday loans. This would be a great opportunity for a community non-profit organization (NPO) to open a loan business that, in turn, financially educates its clients to manage their finances to eliminate the need for payday loans. Any profits could pay the employees and other expenses while using a lower percentage to sustain the NPO.

CHAPTER 11

CREDIT IMPORTANCE

BLUF—Importance of Credit

- ◆ Credit Defined (What is it?)
- ◆ Debt Load
- ◆ How to Build Good Credit
- ◆ Importance of Good Credit
- ◆ Why You Need Credit Cards
- ◆ Debit Cards

Credit is essentially the balance in a person's favor in an account. In personal relationships, one is viewed as having a positive relationship if they are viewed as doing ten good or positive things to each bad or negative thing. In the world of finances, the rules differ.

A financial institution, like a bank, may view my credit based on the funds I have deposited in their institution, concrete items that I own (home, business, or property), and my debt load. Your financial transactions outside the system will not count towards your credit report score.

Here's an easy way to look at a **debt load.** Let's say I purchased a home for $100,000 and still have a $40,000 mortgage with a financial institution on that home. (Mortgage is a fancy word for an owed debt.) The financial institution may well be interested in loaning me up to 80% of my ownership ($48,000). That $48,000 is 80% of my $60,000 of equity (0.8 times $60,000). The other factors are that I have a source of income and not many other unpaid debts (credit cards, car notes, consumer loans, etc.). Get into a habit of knowing your income-to-debt ratio.

So how does one **build good credit**? A FICO score is calculated using many pieces of credit data from your credit report. Yes, your legal transactions are documented in a credit report. The following five factors account for your credit score: payment history (35%), amounts owed (30%), length of credit history (15%), new credit (10%), and credit mix (10%). You can do some homework and visit a site like Experian.com to find out what is considered a good credit score.

FICO was originally Fair, Isaac and Company. To learn the history behind this credit reporting score, you can google FICO. Building good credit is vital since most people are not in a position to purchase a home, car, or even major appliances without credit. Good credit equates to money (cash) in that it saves you money.

Why is **credit important**? Credit is the opportunity to use other people's money based on you paying it back to them in the future with interest. You are very fortunate if you can obtain a no-interest loan. A "best practice" is to pay off that no-interest loan within the agreement's timeframe to avoid paying excessive financial penalties. That is why it is important to have good credit and maintain it.

Good credit equates to money. You can do two things to maintain a good credit score: pay all of your bills on time and never use more than 30% of your available credit. My personal goal is to use no more than 20% of my available credit.

I believe everyone needs at least two **credit cards**. Some people are against owning any credit cards because they have accumulated so much wealth that they do not feel a need to use them. They can pay for everything in cash or its equivalents. You, I, and most people are not in that position.

If you own a credit card, ensure that you have a rewards card. Use it along with a loyalty card to save money on your purchases. Visit a site like Bankrate.com to find the credit card that provides rewards that meet your needs.

Now, I do have a pet peeve. Personally, I'm not too fond of **debit cards**. Why? Because your money comes directly out of your account, and you have less power to dispute a purchase than if you used a credit card. Yet, the silver lining is that you can cyber-securely pay your bills through your financial institution's bill pay method. That, in turn, automatically balances your financial statement.

CHAPTER 12

STREAMS OF INCOME

BLUF—Streams of Income

- ◆ Income Defined
- ◆ 8 Categories/Sources of Income
- ◆ Banked vs. Unbanked
- ◆ Rule of 72
- ◆ Streams of Income vs. Stagnant Streams

Income is best defined as money regularly received through work, investments, or other means. Streams of income refer to several types that are flowing to you.

It has been said that the average millionaire has at least six different streams of income. Ecclesiastes 11:2 (NIV): *Invest in seven ventures, yes, in eight; you do not know what disaster may come upon the land.*

Eight different categories of income include the following:

1. Earned income obtained as an employee.
2. Profit income earned from buying and selling products.
3. Interest income gained from lending money.
4. Dividend income earned through owning stocks (equities) of companies.
5. Rental income earned from renting out properties.
6. Capital gains income earned through the sales of appreciated assets.
7. Residual income earned when a job is done, and you still get paid.
8. Royalty income.

As a caveat to income streams, please note that an appreciated asset is any asset that has increased in value, such as a stock or real estate. Typical examples of residual income are book or music sales. To me, royalty income is a subset of residual income in that it is earned through someone else selling your ideas. An example of royalty income is the payment received from one of my previous books currently being sold through Amazon's platform.

Most Americans with a job have **banked** accounts in a financial institution that provide two sources of income. That would be their job and an interest-bearing financial account like a savings and/or checking account. You cannot easily and legally build financial wealth if you have a job and are **unbanked**.

Action Item: Your mission for this week is to open a brokerage (financial) account to invest in the stock market with mutual funds, stocks, or both. Ensure that you have some dividend-paying mutual funds and stocks. That one move will give you three sources of income. Note that dividends and interest are passive forms of income. Passive income grows your wealth while you sleep.

Please be aware of the **Rule of 72**. In a nutshell, dividing 72 by your annual rate of return gives you the number of years it will take for your money to double. For example, if I invest $100 with a guaranteed return of 8% per year, my money will double in nine years (72 divided by 8% annual yield earned). Simple math is needed to follow your money.

Down the road, when you sell any of those appreciated assets, you have produced capital gain income, giving you four sources of income. The largest asset that most people acquire is their home. Homeownership is a foundation for building financial wealth. You can borrow against it, and when you sell it, the bulk of those capital gains may land on your lap tax-free. We will discuss this topic more later. The IRS even allows you to rent your home for two weeks per year without having to report that income.

If you have any product or service you can sell at a profit, you have now generated a fifth stream of income—profit income. Do this by starting a side hustle in an area of interest. You can write and sell books, give paid speeches, be a caterer, build and design websites, tutor students, provide child care, pet care, and many more.

Finally, if you are blessed to rent out any property (real estate), you now have rental income and up to six streams of income! Think Airbnb for renting out your home, rental cars, storage units, and more.

I refer to **streams of income**. Why streams? A pool of water that is **stagnant** produces no life. Likewise, a moving stream of water allows for life and the purification of the water. Hiding your money in your mattress or a safety deposit box produces no income. Stagnant money rarely—if ever—produces an increase. Strive to keep your money moving in profitable investments to grow it, protect it in safe investments, or use it to uplift (buildup) your community.

CHAPTER 13

MIDDLE CLASS: THE
IMPORTANCE OF FAVOR

BLUF—Streams of Income

- ◆ Are You in the Middle Class?
- ◆ Attributes of Being in the Middle Class
- ◆ God's Favor

---

re you a member of the **middle class**? Google "what income is considered middle class," and you will see a variety of responses based on the U.S. city or state where you reside, along with the size of your family. The answer is not always solely based on income.

If you live in the U.S. and have $10 million debt free, you are definitely middle class—probably wealthy. Likewise, you are wealthy if you have $50 million and are $2 million in debt. You are truly wealthy at

$75 million and above with minimal debt. What if you make $50,000 per year, have $750,000 in savings, have no debt, and live off $30,000 per year? It depends and can go either way based on your age and other conditions. I forgot who made this comment, but they said James Harden and Tom Brady are rich, but Jeff Bezos and Oprah Winfrey are wealthy.

Let's get back to the middle class. The Pew Research Center defined middle-income adults in 2021 as those with an annual household income that was two-thirds to double the national median income in 2020. After income adjustment for household size, the middle-class income is about $52,000 to $156,000 annually in 2020 for a household of three.

Personally, I believe the opportunity to be in the middle-class kicks in typically at about the $35 and above hourly rate. I stress the word "opportunity" because it depends on the cost of living for where you live and what debt load one carries.

What are some **attributes of being middle class**? Six attributes follow:
1. Own a home
2. Able to afford to educate your kids through a trade school or college
3. Able to take off and pay for a family vacation (a family reunion, wedding, or funeral is not a vacation)
4. Can pay your bills on time
5. Have a secure source of income
6. Can save and grow money

If you can do the above and have a manageable debt load while maintaining your health and the health of your familial relationships, you are blessed and favored to be a member of the middle class. You can have great character attributes of hard work, grit, self-discipline, honesty, and be thrifty and aspirational—however, that is a values discussion versus a financial wealth discussion.

At the end of the day, we are an accident or health emergency away from financial well-being. Sometimes we need **God's favor**. We are looking at moving beyond the middle class to building generational wealth to support our family and communities.

CHAPTER 14

SAVINGS AND INVESTMENT (OPTIONS AND INSTRUMENTS)

BLUF—Savings and Investments

- ♦ Savings and Investing Options
- ♦ Tax Savings Investment Options
- ♦ Real Estate
- ♦ Blockchain
- ♦ Volatility

There are a variety of instruments to save your money. A brief description of a few of the most common ones and some of the trendy newer ones will follow. All of these instruments present an investment opportunity. However, the savings option is traditionally more short-term in nature. Short-term and less risk generally means your rate of return is much less—say, fewer than 3%. That means if I save or invest $100 with an annual return of 3%, I end up with $103 at the end of the year, for a gain of only $3.00.

Now we cannot consistently give to the poor or tithe unless we live within our means. Refer to Proverbs 24:27 (NIV): *Put your outdoor work in order and get your fields ready; after that, build your house.* That scripture will come in handy or be timelier when we get into protecting our assets.

Savings and Investment Options

Your short-term options are typically limited to savings accounts, money market accounts, and certificates of deposit (CD). One may even consider **Treasury Inflation Protection Securities** (TIPS).

A **simple savings account** is most common and is generally offered through banks and credit unions. It is a liquid form of investment in which deposits are backed up by the Federal Deposit Insurance Corporation (FDIC) to $250,000.

A **money market account** typically earns a higher rate of return than a simple savings account. It may have a higher minimum balance requirement and limited check writing and debit withdrawal features. These accounts offer the same FDIC protections as the simple savings account.

A **certificate of deposit (CD)** is similar to a savings account. However, it has a time deposit feature called a maturity date. The maturity date usually ranges from 30 days to 5 years with a specific fixed interest rate. For illustration purposes, I lock in a 5% annual rate on $100 for two years. After one year, I will have $105, and after two years, I will have $110.25. If I withdraw early, I may lose a portion of the interest.

Once you get beyond the readily accessible cash, you get to the medium (five years) to long-term (ten-plus years) savings options. Now you are looking at stocks (common and preferred), American Depositary Receipts (ADRs), bonds (corporate and government), Exchange Traded

Funds (ETF), and mutual funds. You can do a bit of legwork or homework to find out what bonds (debt instruments), stocks or equities (investments in businesses), and pooled investments (mutual funds and ETFs) there are. More risky investments include options, futures, and even collectibles. These types of investments go into the tax-saving options that follow.

Tax Savings Investment Options

The investing and tax saving options include Traditional Individual Retirement Accounts (IRA), ROTH IRA, 401(k), 403(b), Simplified Employee Pension (SEP), and Health Savings Account (HSA). There are probably more options than these.

A **Traditional Individual Retirement Account (IRA)** allows one to accumulate tax-deferred money in a personal savings account. Limits on annual contributions allowed depend on your personal and/or spouse's income levels. The earnings are also taxed when used. Consult a tax professional or educate yourself about this opportunity, as you may have age-based withdrawal conditions on these financial options.

A **ROTH IRA** is similar to the traditional IRA, yet it offers an advantage in that while you pay taxes on the money that goes into the account, your future withdrawals are tax-free. There are annual contribution limits, and you may tap your contributions tax-free and penalty-free anytime over age 59 and a half after meeting a 5-year holding requirement. In all cases, it would be wise to seek the sage counsel of a tax professional.

A **401(k)** or **Thrift Savings Plan** (federal government) is an employer-sponsored retirement plan. The employee can save and invest a portion of their paycheck before taxes are taken out, and your employer may match employee contributions to a certain level of their pay (an example is 5%). The good news is that the annual contributions are much higher than the previously mentioned types of IRAs. Please note that some plans, such as the federal Thrift Savings Plan (TSP), recently incorporated a ROTH IRA (pre-tax option) within the investment options that may differ in its contribution requirements when compared to a separate ROTH IRA. Again, please consult the wise counsel of a tax professional.

A **Simplified Employee Pension (SEP)** is a retirement vehicle that allows an employer to contribute to a Traditional IRA (SEP IRA) for each eligible employee. The limits on the employer contributions to the SEP IRA are much higher than the prior mentioned types of IRAs. These are good plans for self-employed people because they have the same contribution limits as profit-sharing plans without complex compliance and reporting rules. It does not allow catch-up provisions for people 50 and older; one must also make a required minimum distribution when they reach the age of 72. Again, consult a tax professional when setting up or participating in this retirement vehicle.

A **Health Savings Account (HSA)** is a medical savings account with tax advantages. The contributions to this account may be withdrawn tax-free for qualified medical expenses: out-of-pocket dental, medical, and vision costs. All funds placed into an HSA are 100% tax deductible. There are limits on how much one may contribute to an HSA annually, though. Consult a tax professional to learn the limits. Also, it does not cover insurance premiums and must be used within two years.

Real Estate

Real estate that consists of purchasing property as an investment (rental income, farming, etc.) can be used for investment and retirement considerations. It is one of the legs of the three-legged stool for making money—people must eat, have a place to stay, and have clothing on their backs. A new area is entertainment as people are now always seeking ways to be entertained.

Blockchain

New options on the scene include **blockchain options** (Bitcoin, COIN, NFTs, etc.). My advice to you is to learn all you can about the options above before jumping into the newer ventures. All investments should work the same— put your cash equivalents or income into the investment vehicle, and when you cash out, you should have your expected rate of return after your taxes and fees are paid.

Never personally invest in something that you—or your financial advisor—do not understand. Vetted and trusted investment advisors may feel comfortable investing in options you do not understand based on their knowledge, expertise, and track record. Also, do not invest all of your funds in one place. Some sage advice that still applies is, "Do not put all of your eggs in one basket." Another term for that is asset allocation.

Volatility

Understand the **volatility** of your investment decisions to better gauge your investment risk appetite (i.e., conservative, moderate, or aggressive). Are you comfortable if your investment goes up or down in value by 5%, 10%, 15%, 20%, or more? That is the volatility under consideration here. Just know that you will rarely reach financial security by placing the bulk of your funds in short-term options like savings, money market accounts, and CDs due to their lower rates of return. The caveat is that it may be a viable option if you come into a great fortune. Ecclesiastes 11:2 (NIV): *Invest in seven ventures, yes, in eight; you do not know what disaster may come upon the land.*

Please revisit Rule of 72 from Chapter 12.

CHAPTER 15

FINANCIAL VAMPIRES

BLUF—Financial Killers

- Medical Debts
- Social Injustice (hidden and in your face)
- Not Maintaining One's Health
- Divorces
- Not Paying Your Taxes
- Improper Insurance Coverage
- Loaning Money
- Overspending
- Inflation and Other

What is a vampire? A vampire is someone (or a situation) that heartlessly preys on others. It could be a blackmailer. In the context of this chapter, it is any person, thing, or situation that sucks your financial life or well-being out of you.

The most common financial vampire is **medical debts**. If one has an expensive long-term or short-term illness that is not adequately covered by insurance, it will wreck your finances. I believe medical bills are the number one reason for people going bankrupt. An advisable course of action is being sure to ask for your medical debt to be forgiven or seek a governmental agency that may be able to assist with this request.

Social injustice is the most pervasive and hidden financial vampire that primarily targets minorities (i.e., Hispanics, Latinos, African Americans, Native Americans, Asian Pacific, and Asian Indians) and other non-represented groups (LGBTQIA+, women, and low-income households).

Some policies incorporate social injustice, are often state sanctioned, and involve the "so-called" –isms of sexism, racism, misogyny, and so forth. Public policies can result in redlining, over-policing in certain communities, voting rights, poor educational and healthcare opportunities, pollution, lack of Internet access, and politicizing the separation of "so-called" races. For example, redlining keeps some minority communities unbanked, depresses property values, and results in poorer educational and health outcomes. That affects one's opportunity to acquire wealth for future generations.

Maintaining your physical, spiritual, and brain **health** is a must. If those areas are not maintained, they will become a financial vampire. Poor diets, lack of rest, and lack of exercise will gradually turn you into a sick person and reduce your days on this planet. A lack of spiritual health will cause you to live in despair and affect your decision-making. You may mistreat others and yourself. Your brain health is essential, as well. So, utilize mental health professionals, clergy (for spiritual), and the like to maintain that aspect of your health. Sync your physical, mental, and spiritual health to live a life of balance.

Divorces are expensive and can be even more costly if children and extensive property are involved. Many have experienced divorce and the resultant spousal support and child support payments. The court does not care about the reason for the divorce; they merely follow the laws and divorce guidelines in their jurisdiction. Divorces differ greatly from state to state in the U.S. Just assume you are splitting half of your resources acquired during the marriage. In addition, one party may pay child support and, in some cases, spousal support. One or both parties may have to find new housing. If you cannot come to mutually agreeable terms, the attorneys will become your mutual financial vampires.

Evasion of state, local, and federal **taxes** can convert into a self-imposed vampire. The late payment fees and other costs associated with not paying your taxes can be very expensive. Some people even do jail time, which does not paint a pretty picture for your financial future.

Improper **insurance coverage** can harm your finances. Getting into a car accident or having a traffic infraction without automobile insurance may also become a pricey endeavor. You may even lose your car and license. Remember never to drive under the influence of alcohol or other drugs.

Not having the appropriate insurance on your home can be costly, as well. Even if you have home insurance, you may not be covered for flood or earthquake damages. Know what you are covered for in this arena by consulting a professional insurance specialist and gauging the risks.

Loaning money you cannot afford to lose is a financial vampire. If the loaned money is not repaid, it may cause financial hardship for the person who loaned it and frayed personal relationships. Proverbs 17:18 (NIV): *One who has no sense shakes hands in pledge and puts up security for a neighbor.* In the past, I have loaned money to friends and family with mixed results when it came time for the person to pay me back.

Another common financial vampire is going into debt to purchase things you cannot afford or **overspending**. Overspending is caused by impulse buying, brain health disorders, gambling, drug use, and other reasons. All embody one trait—not living within one's financial means.

There are many other financial vampires like **inflation**. Inflation is like high blood pressure—it is the silent killer of your finances. Many of the powerful and wealthy pay the media, legislative, judicial, and regulatory powers to keep the bulk of society poor and divided with the fear of scarcity.

This list was not meant to be all-inclusive. Can you think of a few other financial vampires?

Exercise: Write down *your* financial vampires.

CHAPTER 16

ASSET PROTECTION

BLUF—Protecting Assets

♦ Insurance
♦ Estate Planning
♦ Financial Planning
♦ Business Organization (legal)

N ow that you have obtained information on some financial tools to gain and grow financial wealth, how do you protect that wealth? We just discussed several financial vampires that impede your life's journey toward creating wealth. So how can you grow that wealth? The Bible alludes to wealth protection in Matthew 25:14 (NIV): *Again, it will be like a man going on a journey, who called his servants and entrusted his wealth to them.*

Insurance

If you are still in your working years, obtain **term life insurance** in case you suffer a permanent human condition called "death." The best course of action is to purchase a 20-year-term life policy at age 25 and a second 20-year-term life policy at age 45. Why? The price of that insurance is reasonable. Some also use the term life insurance as a form of wealth creation. For example, let's say my net worth is $200,000, and I have a $1 million term life insurance policy. In the case of my premature death, my family's wealth would increase to $1.2 million. That is where the phrase *"worth more dead than alive"* probably originated.

I favor term life insurance over the other life insurance options. However, there is value in other forms of life insurance that may fit your individual needs. Again, consult an independent insurance specialist and financial planner for information and guidance on various life insurance products. For your needs, visit policygenius.com or newyorklife.com to evaluate the pros and cons of the different life insurance products (e.g., Whole Life, Variable Universal Life, and Universal Life).

Health insurance coverage for you and your family is a no-brainer. Obtain the appropriate coverage you can afford and visit regularly scheduled dental, eye, physical, and mental health appointments. And be intentional. Actually go to your medical providers for regular care. For example, I have my daughters on my health insurance plan, and they can stay on it until age 26 because of the Affordable Care Act.

Another form of insurance is **disability insurance**, which protects your stream of income if you incur a qualified disability that prevents you from earning a living. It is based on your marketable skills, of course. The longer this insurance is in force, the more expensive it becomes.

Please note that many policies have a waiting period from 30, 60, and up to 365 days before your disability benefits start. For example, my waiting period for my disability insurance policy is six months. Check your Social Security benefits to see if you qualify for disability coverage. And utilize gap insurance if applicable. By now, this may sound like a broken record, but please consult your insurance specialist for more information about this form of insurance.

Several other insurances protect against property loss and liability. The different categories of property insurance include auto, motorcycle, all-terrain vehicle (ATV), recreational vehicle (RV), boat, homeowners, renters, condo, co-op, mobile home, personal umbrella, flood, overseas, business owners, and professional liability insurance. You can even get insurance in the categories of sump pump overflow, roof replacement, matching siding coverage, and personal items (jewelry). You'd be surprised what you come across when you do the proper research!

The aforementioned insurance falls into two distinct categories: **property** and **liability**, and a combination of the two. Most people have some sort of dwelling insurance, and if they own any vehicles, they also have insurance for those. The common ones for middle-class families are auto and home or renters. Both protect against property loss and offer opportunities to cover personal liability. Note that some policies directly address business owners and professionals.

Another form of insurance against liability is a **personal umbrella insurance** policy, primarily a liability protection policy that goes into effect if someone gets injured on your property. It can also offer additional protection to your car or other vehicle insurance. It can cover property damage, personal liabilities, and certain lawsuits. Insurance specialists have told me that medical physicians (doctors) are often recommended to get this insurance to offer additional protection. When people learn that you are a doctor, they believe you have a lot of money; they see you as a honey or money pot.

Long-term Care (LTC) Insurance protects your family (spouse, children, and others) from the high costs of end-of-life care, which can run about $100,000 per year. If you have this insurance, it pays the bulk of your late-life health care without you having to use your home as a pledge to cover those expenses. LTC insurance protects your family from those expenses and helps maintain your financial wealth for the next generation. I have an LTC insurance policy.

I am sure there are other boutique forms of insurance that I have not covered. I have used the word "boutique" to signify that there are specialized forms of insurance that are not common. One example is a hand model insuring their hands against injury. Educate yourself on the many ways to protect yourself.

Estate Planning:

The best way to secure or protect your assets is through **estate planning**. That is done through setting up a **Trust** that contains your will, advanced health care directives such as a **Medical** or **Health Care Power of Attorney (POA)**, **Financial POA**, and plans for your last rites (burial, cremation, home-going plans). One may desire to be cremated (burned to ashes) or be buried in a casket (in the ground or above land in a mausoleum). Please note that when you sit down to set all these plans up, the hardest exercise you will ever have is writing your eulogy (which means "good news"). It is a tough exercise—unless you are a narcissist.

Trust: I recommend you educate yourself about the two most common types of trust: **revocable** and **irrevocable**. There are other types of trusts: living and testamentary. I set up a revocable trust that allows me to modify or cancel it during my lifetime. A married couple may create an irrevocable trust to avoid probate and minimize federal estate taxes. However, that trust type is set in stone. Learn the pros and cons of the various trusts by consulting a trusts attorney before proceeding down this road.

The bottom line is that trusts are great tools to transfer wealth and control taxes. Items that can go into a trust are non-retirement accounts, brokerage accounts, non-qualified annuities, cash, certificates of stocks and bonds, life insurance, business interest, and even tangible personal property. Also, a trust offers some protection against creditors and lawsuits. A trust is sometimes just as effective as a marriage **prenuptial**

agreement. That alone should give you enough curiosity to schedule an appointment with a qualified trusts attorney.

Financial Planning:

Talk to a **certified financial planner** about other tools and strategies to use, build up, and transfer your wealth during your lifetime and protect your wealth for your current family and future generations. Please consider taxes and strategies like endowments, land trusts, annuities, and others in your estate and financial planning. For example, I set up an endowment fund with The Dayton Foundation to pass along charitable gifts upon my passing.

Business Legal Organization:

How you set up your business operations can play a major role in protecting your finances. Make sure you choose wisely how you are organized: Limited Liability Corporation (LLC), Sole Owner, Partnership, or Corporation. Be sure you seek the appropriate professionals to help you make the right decision. A later chapter will cover those professionals.

To close, when you become well-off or wealthy, you will have more tools at your disposal. You will then be able to use legal entities, trusts, corporate laws, partnerships, and tax loopholes (options) to maintain and grow your wealth. That is a good problem to have.

CHAPTER 17

RETIREMENT

BLUF—Retirement Considerations

- ♦ What's Your Number?
- ♦ Sources of Income (money)
- ♦ Start Planning Today (Rule of 72)
- ♦ Poem, "The Bridge Builder"
- ♦ Retirement Considerations

Now you are coming up to your retirement years. How does one plan for retirement? I always say one should have their number. **Your number** may be $500,000 by age 65; another may require $2 million. That extra zero makes a big difference. For example, there is a big difference in having $10 and $100, and the amount in between keeps growing as those numbers increase in magnitude. For example, look at the difference between $10,000 and $100,000 vs. $100 and $1,000.

Your retirement can be based on several legs (**sources of income**). Those who have worked for the federal government may have a pension or 401(k) plan, social security, another supplement (annuity), and personal savings. Other public service employees, like teachers, may have a 403(b), better known as a tax-sheltered annuity plan. Likewise, those who retire from the military can add their military retirement to that equation and any disability benefits. My late Uncle Ed had at least three retirement streams of income—military, post office, and educator.

Poor is the person that never paid into a pension, 401(k), 403(b), or SEP during their work years. They may have to rely on social security or its equivalent if they qualify to receive it and on whatever resources they have saved. About 96% of retired Americans qualify for social security benefits. Yet, these benefits are not always available to everyone since many public service employees have their own pension plan (e.g., educators, firefighters, law enforcement). In many cases, this poor person that never contributed to a pension or other retirement plan will never be able to afford to retire unless they have saved up enough resources. I have run across people who tell me that they plan to die on the job and never retire.

To return to the initial plan, **know your number**. The best time to plan for retirement is when you are young, and hopefully unmarried and without children. If you do not have that opportunity, still plan. **START TODAY!** It is easier to save for retirement over 30 to 40 years than to wait until your last 5 to 10 years to start planning for retirement. Why? The **Rule of 72** that we discussed earlier does not have enough time to work for you to build up your wealth if you wait until 5 to 10 years before your retirement to start saving.

Other retirement options are to sell your business or intellectual property or have a stream of funds from rental income. There are many ways to set up your retirement. This is where a great financial planner can benefit you.

A favorite poem of mine that I learned when pledging into my fraternity at Florida Agricultural and Mechanical University (FAMU), Tallahassee, FL., is The Bridge Builder. We actually pledged in those former days, and now it is called an intake process—due to legal liability.

<u>The Bridge Builder</u> by William Allen Dromgoole

An old man going a lone highway,
Came, at the evening cold and gray,
To a chasm vast and deep and wide.
Through which was flowing a sullen tide
The old man crossed in the twilight dim,
The sullen stream had no fear for him;
But he turned when safe on the other side
And built a bridge to span the tide.
"Old man," said a fellow pilgrim near,
"You are wasting your strength with building here;
Your journey will end with the ending day,
You never again will pass this way;
You've crossed the chasm, deep and wide,
Why build this bridge at evening tide?"
The builder lifted his old gray head;
"Good friend, in the path I have come," he said,
"There followed after me to-day
A youth whose feet must pass this way.
This chasm that has been as naught to me
To that fair-haired youth may a pitfall be;
He, too, must cross in the twilight dim;
Good friend, I am building this bridge for him!"

Source: *Father: An Anthology of Verse* (EP Dutton & Company, 1931)

The dual message behind this poem is that we are to plan our lives for the present and future generations. The Bible tells us that a good man leaves an inheritance for their children and their children's children. Focus on the last lines of the three stanzas of the poem.

- ◆ *And built a bridge to span the tide. (wealth transfer)*
- ◆ *Why build this bridge at evening tide?" (moving on)*
- ◆ *I am building this bridge for him!" (future generations)*

A chart shows how an accumulated or one-time $10,000, $50,000, and $200,000 investment would grow from age 28 to 100 at an annual rate of 6%. The one-time investment should double every 12 years.

Age	Cumulative Amount (Rule of 72)		
28	$10,000	$50,000	$200,000
40	$20,000	$100,000	$400,000
52	$40,000	$200,000	$800,000
64	$80,000	$400,000	$1,600,000
76	$160,000	$800,000	$3,200,000
88	$320,000	$1,600,000	$6,400,000
100	$640,000	$3,200,000	$12,800,000

The issue really boils down to the question: *Do I have the ability to live off of my passive income versus having to live off of my earned income?* The answer to that question is generational wealth used wisely.

Retirement:

Let's return to the start of your retirement. **What must one consider?** When do you plan to retire? Where do you plan to retire? Do you plan to retire alone or with another? What will you do with your time (travel, hobbies, other)? Do you have the resources (income) to retire comfortably? Your retirement income sources may include your personal savings, employer pension, social security, home, and other means. How will you obtain health care (out of pocket, Medicare at age 65, Medicare

Prescription Drug Program, Medigap Policy)? Do you have LTC insurance? On average, it can easily cost $100,000 per year in the U.S. for nursing home care. So, obtain LTC insurance at the appropriate age to manage that risk unless one has enough assets to cover those expenses.

Another major consideration before heading into retirement is the status of your health. Did you take a medical retirement? Are you completely healthy for your age? Do people in your family typically live to their 90s or pass away in their mid-70s? That will give you a good estimate of how many years you need to plan for retirement (life expectancy). The two biggest retirement fears are running out of money and being in poor health.

As civilians working for the Air Force, we have a plan, do, check, and act (PDCA) process. Before you retire, I suggest you do a dry run. Assess your financial requirements, consider risks to your streams of income (inflation, market risks, etc.), estimate your expense in retirement (to include taxes), and do a simulated dry run with your sources of income based on what you expect to receive from your social security, pension, annuity, or other employment-related sources. Some financial planners believe that one needs 60-90% of pre-retirement income in retirement. Then determine if there is an income gap. For instance, you may feel you are short of your goals by $15,000 per year. Two ways to resolve that are to work for an additional period of time to accumulate more assets or plan to work part-time after you retire. There are other options, as well. For example, one may reduce their planned retirement expenses or use their home as a source of income.

The order of withdrawal of assets in retirement can vary. An annuity, which is an insurance product, can convert your pension to pay you as a single-life annuity or as a qualified joint and survivor annuity (QJSA). The annuity will give you a stream of income throughout your life or a set period per the terms of the agreement. Be sure to consult with independent financial planning professionals on converting your pension to an annuity as opposed to taking your pension as a lump sum. Some financial planners urge you to take tax-deferred withdrawals first to reduce taxes (i.e., draw from your IRA) and then withdraw your income from your tax-exempt source (Roth IRA). Finally, draw from your taxable accounts. Again, consult with your financial advisors on this matter. Additional sources of income include your home, other real property, and cash-value life insurance policies.

Finally, if you reach age 65, you get Medicare. If you are lucky enough to reach age 72, the Required Minimum Distribution (RMD) comes into play for those with 401(k) and 403(b) accounts. Our U.S. Congress can choose to adjust that age with a change in laws. If you do not take the RMD, you are subject to a 50% penalty from the IRS. There is no lifetime RMDs for a Roth IRA. The RMD allows you to transfer generational wealth and give excess funds to charities.

CHAPTER 18

GENERATIONAL WEALTH OPPORTUNITIES

BLUF—Generational Wealth Creators

- ◆ Degrees that Produce High Earnings
- ◆ Top 10 Jobs that Make One Rich
- ◆ Education 529 Plans
- ◆ Life Insurance
- ◆ Your Home (Real Property)
- ◆ Assets from 8 Streams of Income

Degrees that lead to high earnings are engineering, math, accounting, computer science, and Master of Business Administration (MBA). Do not forget or neglect the non-college degree options like electricians and plumbers. Today, the certification opportunities are in Information Technology, Cybersecurity, Software, and other emerging areas. Being a business owner can be lucrative in the right market, and being a franchise owner may be right for you. However, do your research and homework.

When looking at the top jobs that make one rich, do not leave out great salespeople across various fields and disciplines. A 2022 Google search of the **top 10 jobs that make one rich** follows:

Doctor	Surgeon
Investment Banker	Corporate Executive
Petroleum Engineer	Psychiatrist
Data Scientist	Lawyer
Research & Development Manager	Dentist

Use educational savings plans, such as **529 Plans,** to educate your family (spouse, children, and grandchildren) and yourself. That education can range from certifications and workshops to college degrees that can lead to higher income opportunities after graduation. That knowledge can help you save and invest to create generational wealth for your family and help build up your community.

We previously discussed how **life insurance** can help create generational wealth. When you die, appropriate life insurance policies will create generational wealth. Is your family better off financially with you dead or alive? Do not ask or answer that question.

Your **home** is a source of generational wealth. How? You can use the equity in your home to invest in yourself and other things. Likewise, if you sell your home, you can use your appreciated capital gains to purchase homes with more value. You have an opportunity to increase your wealth with each transaction. That home can, in turn, be left to your children or grandchildren—or you can cash out of that home to earn significantly tax-free gains.

Based on <u>usafacts.org</u>, the 2019 U.S. homeownership rate for all races was 64.6%. It was 42.1% for Black Americans compared to 73.3% for Whites. All other races were below 64.6%.

Story:

When I planned to purchase my home, my main objective was to find a space to live in that could also be a future investment opportunity. I looked at factors such as the quality of the neighborhood school system, daily commute, neighborhood amenities, property taxes, prior land use history, age of development, Homeowners Association fees, and affordability. Were the neighbors warm and inviting? Did they maintain their property?

No matter how much money you make, it does you no good if you spend all of it and create debt. It is not what you make that creates wealth; it's what you save and invest that creates wealth. If you win the lottery and have no financial education or cultural background on what to do with the money, you will blow it and end up in a worse situation than before. You will be broke, depressed, have broken relationships, and be disappointed.

One of the best ways to become wealthy is to become a business owner. It is hard work. Yet, it provides one with many more opportunities to create wealth as opposed to simply being a wage employee. However, not everyone is meant to be a business owner, so know thyself and your limitations before taking the leap. Your paycheck as an employee or independent consultant may actually be your route to building generational wealth.

Story:

My mother and father were K-12 educators. During their lifetime, they built a home, raised two sons, and fostered a vegetable garden every year. My father worked side jobs, which primarily paid for his sons' college educations. My parents were charitable in their community and saved their money. They lived life and amassed a decent sum of money over their lifetime. Some of their real property and funds went to their children, grandchildren, and even great-grandchildren. They each benefited from their parents' upraising.

Use as many of the **8 streams of income** to build your wealth over your lifetime. Those 8 streams of income are:

1. Earned income obtained as an employee.
2. Profit income earned from buying and selling products.
3. Interest income gained from lending money.
4. Dividend income earned through owning stocks (equities) of companies.
5. Rental income earned from renting out properties.
6. Capital gains income earned through the sales of appreciated assets.
7. Residual income earned when a job is done, and you still get paid.
8. Royalty income.

Time is your friend in building and sustaining wealth.

CHAPTER 19

USE PROFESSIONALS

BLUF—Financial Professional Roles
◆ Certified Public Accountants (CPAs)
◆ Professional Tax Planners
◆ Certified Financial Planners
◆ Realtors and Real Estate Attorneys
◆ Other Attorneys
◆ Other Professionals

One of the things I highlighted to my daughters at a very young age was that the best athletes in the world all tend to use **professional trainers**. Tiger Woods and Tom Brady each have a coach. Chief Executive Officers (CEO) have certified life **coaches** and personal consultants to improve their performance. My primary physician (medical doctor) even has his own doctor.

You can be stingy with your cash and try to do everything yourself, but you may not get ahead. Years ago, I contracted with a caterer (Mr. Dixon in Dayton, Ohio). He informed me that he hired the best servers and staff; he ensured they were professional and paid well. Why? He could do the job without them. However, he could do more business and make more money by hiring qualified assistance or talent. Don't try to do everything yourself!

Certified Public Accountants (CPAs) and professional tax preparers are key to your ability to sustain any appreciable wealth you gain. When I was younger, I did my own taxes. They were simple, and I had time on my hands to do them. As I acquired more assets, I learned that having a trained professional handle my taxes saved me time and money. Why? Because the trained tax professional was better and more efficient than me. They actually saved me money and helped me grow my assets based on their expertise.

A few years ago, I utilized the services of a **certified financial planner**. They helped me forecast what my savings and investments would grow to over several years. With that information, they figured out where I would be at age 60, age 62, age 65, age 67, age 70, and up to 100. They took into consideration my social security, IRA's, 401(k), and other accounts. I was even encouraged to get Long Term Care (LTC) Insurance, which I did. The LTC insurance will take pressure off my family as caregivers in the future if it is required. Extremely wealthy people can cancel LTC insurance.

Realtors are important when purchasing any property. It could be your personal home, rental property, or other real estate. You should also hire a good **real estate attorney** to look at those purchases. With attorneys, always hire (retain) the best ones you can afford. That simple act will save you many headaches in the long run. Referrals are a best practice when it comes to hiring professionals.

When you do not have much, you can manage your own investments using basic investment strategies. However, if you do not have the time to do your own investing, you should hire a relevant financial professional. There are major investment firms like Merrill Lynch, Morgan Stanley, Schwab, Raymond James, and a variety of others. There are also qualified independent financial professionals. You can use robo-advisors, an automated platform that manages your investments. Examples include Wealthfront and Betterment. You can invest with Schwab and Fidelity on your own. I do a combination of managing my own accounts and having a couple of large firms manage the bulk of my finances. Build a **team**.

You may need a bevy of **attorneys** to handle your affairs (real estate, estate planning, and other matters) over your lifetime. Estate attorneys that focus on trusts and the contents therein were discussed in earlier chapters.

If you are in real estate, you need home inspectors, plumbers, electricians, landscapers, and other related professionals. Again, build your team.

The **bottom line** is for you to put a team of qualified professionals around you to help create and protect your generational wealth-producing assets. Do not try to do everything on your own.

CHAPTER 20

SELF-STRESS TEST

BLUF—Financial Stress Test

- ◆ Nest Egg for 6-12 Months, Plus
- ◆ Divorce
- ◆ Disability
- ◆ Major Unplanned Events/Expense
- ◆ Estate Planning Checkup

B efore you experience a life transition (e.g., death, divorce, job loss, medical crisis), it is prudent to stress test your financial plan.

First, do you have enough money to make it 6 months, 9 months, or 12 months without a job? Depending on your stage of life, you may need a nest egg that provides enough money to live off for more than a year. **Solution**: If not, put a plan in place to make this situation right.

Second, if you were to divorce or split from a partner, would you and your former spouse or partner continue to thrive? Or will each of you face major financial setbacks? **Solution**: This one is tricky, as you can both be living within your means, but a divorce or separation could set you both back. Please note that you may have to agree to monitor each other's credit to avoid hidden debt surprises.

Third, if the chief breadwinner suffered a disability, could your family survive financially for six months? A year? Three years? Five years? **Solution**: Put plans in effect to cover this scenario to the best of your ability. A possible solution is disability insurance, which gets more expensive with age.

Fourth, if your car died or your furnace went out in the middle of winter and had to be replaced, could you do so without experiencing a major financial setback? **Solution**: Again, you must have resources set aside to handle unexpected emergencies. Make a plan to address this matter. It could be home appliance insurance protection, increased cash reserves in your budget, or a low-interest line of credit.

Fifth, will your estate planning (trusts, wills, and POA) work if you were in a car accident and unconscious for 45 days? Or even died?

Solution: The fifth one is an important stress test. Check to see if your Healthcare POA and Finance POA will be recognized so that your loved ones have access to your relevant financial accounts (savings, checking, investment accounts, retirement accounts, educational savings accounts, insurance, Health Savings Account, etc.). They should also be able to access your pertinent **passwords.** This is probably the toughest one to gauge and probably the most important. Many have resolved to save passwords on paper in a secure location rather than stored on an inaccessible phone or computer.

Story:

When my mother and father died, my brother and I had no clue about how many financial accounts they had beyond their standard banking and employee retirement accounts. Additionally, both of my parents were in the last two years of their life while I was in the middle of a divorce in another state. They could not adequately communicate their assets to my brother and me. My name was on various accounts, such as joint, Payable on Death (POD), and others. I lived in Ohio, whereas they lived in Georgia. Therefore, distance and their inability to share information on their financial accounts were barriers. I had no idea what my parents owned and did not find out about some debts and financial accounts until almost over a year after they passed. Hospitals were the worst collectors of debt to deal with. That was one of the reasons I decided to write this book—to get one to think about those particular items before one found themselves in the same situation.

Story:

Likewise, when my good friend, Richard R. Napier, Sr., passed, his surviving wife and children had to search his various accounts. The good news was that he listed his wife on the bulk of his accounts. When Richard and I talked about writing this book, he reflected on the many things he needed to do and got it done.

CHAPTER 21

FINAL THOUGHTS, A PLAN

Generating Wealth

Generating wealth must be a life-long process to change your family's culture. Define your purpose, make it family-centered, focus on life-long learning by using professionals, and revisit the topic periodically. Make this process fun and a part of your routine as automatic as breathing. And it should not be a tedious exercise.

Now that we have figured out our needs versus wants, paid off debts, and established our emergency fund, we are ready to generate wealth. If you purchase large ticket items like a home, you can pay it off over time and generate wealth. Likewise, you can also ensure your children's education is taken care of. We can (prioritize) do more than one thing at once.

First, tackle your retirement. Let's say your family's annual income is $50,000. You ideally at a minimum want to have 25 times that amount saved, which equals $1.25 Million. A 4% draw off that amount annually will provide you with $50,000. Let's assume you have a pension, social security, or another post-retirement source that provides you with $15,000. Then you would only need to save $875,000 to meet that goal. Please note that these are general guidelines professional financial planners advocate, not investment advice.

How do we generate those funds? One possible solution is to save a minimum of 15% of your gross income and invest it in the stock market via mutual funds, ETFs, and/or individual stocks. An example stock portfolio is to invest in:

- ◆ Growth
- ◆ Growth and Income
- ◆ Aggressive Growth
- ◆ International

For example, one could start off with equal weights in each fund at the beginning of their career. As one gets closer to retirement, bond and income funds become more appropriate for retirement savings funds protection. Again, contact a professional financial advisor for guidance that will fit your individualized needs.

Assume your funds will return 7-8% annually for planning purposes; the stock market has traditionally returned 11-12% per year. I use 6% returns for my planning purposes.

If this is the case, once you have achieved your retirement goal of $1.25 million, it is now time to generate wealth for future generations. That is done by living within your means, investing more of your funds into the stock market, and diversifying into other investments (real estate, a business, or other opportunities).

Please note that the airlines tell you to put on your oxygen mask first in case of an emergency before placing one on your children. I suggest you follow that same guidance and make taking care of retirement a priority before fully funding your children's college education or other educational funds. Then move forward with growing your generational wealth.

Do this by continuing to invest in the stock market, private investments, rental properties, blockchain investments, non-fungible tokens (NFTs), business ownership like franchise investments, and other relevant ones. Name, image, and likeness (NIL) is a new financial wealth-producing opportunity. Look it up.

A great goal for the next generation is a paid-off education and a 10-to-25-year head start on saving for their retirement. When I retire and eventually expire, I would love to be able to be in a position to leave my family $1 million or more with which they can build upon (a combination of paid-off property, cash equivalents, equities, royalties, and more).

Assume that a generation is 25 years. It may take your family 2 to 5 generations to produce generational wealth. As my grandfather, Lee Moore, Sr., said, "It takes a generation to build up wealth and a generation to destroy it." Do not be selfish and only think of self; think of your family and community. Also, if you are starting the culture in your family to produce wealth and you are in debt, think 40 to 125 years into the future (yet, build the culture just in case someone hits the cosmic lottery).

To grow wealth in any area, do the following:
1. Visualize your desired goal (e.g., $2.5M assets with $1.75M liquid).
2. Write down your goals in sufficient detail. Be specific; write meaningful yet achievable goals (e.g., write three books over the next five years). Your actions must be relevant & time-bound (e.g., sell 250,000 books, each book providing a $4 profit). Evaluate your progress and adjust as needed (e.g., my quarterly progress may not be linear).
3. Take disciplined action to achieve.
4. Reap what you sow daily.
5. Undergird the process with faith in God.

My roadmap to generational wealth is:

- ♦ God is my source.
- ♦ First provisions go to God at 10% or more.
- ♦ Live within my means and have a budget.
- ♦ Records are a must.
- ♦ Spend wisely and put aside (encumber, save) funds.
- ♦ Be content with God's provisions (but not lazy).
- ♦ Invest to grow your wealth (legal financial system).
- ♦ Place appropriate professionals on your team.
- ♦ Build a family culture of life-long financial learning.
- ♦ Make it fun.
- ♦ Different strategies are required for different levels.

When I say different strategies are required for different levels, I mean it takes different strategies to manage $50,000 versus $500,000, $2 million, $25 million, or $100 million.

Start thinking beyond tomorrow, and seek to have a 1-year, 3-year, 5-year, 10-year, 25-year, 50-year, and even a 100-year plan for your family. Consult relevant professionals for your team to build your generational wealth: insurance agents, CPAs, financial advisors (investment, retirement, and financial planners), and attorneys (real estate, tax, business, trust, wills, etc.). Hire these professionals from within your community when you can. Include charitable foundations in your planning. For example, I have charitable accounts in The Dayton Foundation and its African American Community Fund.

Financial Accounts: Banking (savings, money market), TIPS, equity (stocks, ETFs), bonds, mutual funds, cryptocurrency, etc.

Insurance Policies: life, home, auto, umbrella, disability, flood, riders, long-term care, other

Business Records: assets, inventory, debts, taxes, other

Material Possessions: homes, rental properties, vehicles, boats, airplanes, farm equipment, jewelry, and more

Miscellaneous: Last 3 years of tax records, debts, other

Plan, do, check, act, and revisit these processes. Along the journey, teach your family and self. Have fun! Life is meant to be enjoyed.

It takes money to make money. The saying that dollars do not grow on trees is not true. Just ask an apple farmer. To be an investor, one must generate free cash flow. Create a "holy shit" fund to avoid tapping into savings when one experiences an emergency.

Be consistent and build your various funds a little bit over time (patience). In the past, I would have recommended that you carry cash unless you can use your credit card like a debit card. If you do use your credit card, always pay it off in full when the bill is due. There are now newer and more secure modes to pay for items/services other than cash; one must change with the times. Avoid paying interest as much as possible. Be intentional in growing your wealth and transferring it.

Epilogue

We have done several things in the previous chapters:

- ◆ We defined generational wealth and financial freedom.
- ◆ We pinpointed the negatives of not benefitting from generational wealth.
- ◆ We discussed how to determine where one (and/or their family) is with regard to their plan to achieve generational wealth.

One must document their current net worth based on what they own and owe.

Set a plan (your BUDGET) to give to charity, spend, save, and invest with the goal of achieving financial freedom. My space flight analogy follows. View financial freedom as the rocket propulsion required to escape Earth's gravitational pull. The generational wealth piece is achieved by your deep space-like journey without an appreciable pull of Earth's gravity (bills/debts).

For the believers in a higher being, there is a spiritual purpose for wealth and the importance of God's favor. Develop the purpose for your income and wealth based on your faith, then budget your priorities. Your budget is the part you can do, and it reveals your priorities for your income and wealth. Keep track of your expenses throughout your lifetime, and be sure to have a "rainy day" fund (emergency fund).

Now that your foundation is set, you are prepared to move forward with knowledge of good and bad debt, debt payoff strategies, and the importance of building and maintaining a good credit score. Culturally, you know what middle-class values are and the attributes that reveal your true status as middle class in the U.S. or your country.

It is time to save and invest using the free cash generated by having more income than debts. There are many financial vampires to avoid or temper along the way. The various income streams are then used to save and invest using a multitude of financial vehicles. There are short-term, intermediate-term, and long-term financial vehicles to save and invest your income. Real estate and other options are available to grow your wealth to live off of, live in, borrow against, educate, donate, and grow generational wealth. At the same time, one is saving for their retirement, dream vacations, hobbies, emergencies, family's education, and other priorities.

Along the way, one has to protect their assets with various insurance products, estate planning, trusts, wills, power of attorney (POA), and more. Use the appropriate legal, insurance, financial planning, tax, realtors, certified public accountant (CPA), and other professionals to grow and protect your wealth. Continuously educate yourself about finances and wealth. Put a team of professionals around you to stay on track.

Remember that the world of the generous gets larger and larger, whereas the world of the selfish gets smaller and smaller. Need I say more?

In a nutshell, do not ask for what you are not prepared to receive and manage. **Do not fall for the "doing nothing is an option."** As T.D. Jakes said, "Get Ready! Get Ready!"

And remember, at the end of the day, when it comes to producing generational wealth, "Doing nothing is an option." But, do not be that person or family. Get started now!

DOCUMENTING YOUR LIFE

Organizing your life falls under three categories.

A Filing System:

Store documents securely by paper, electronically, or both. Use a fireproof filing cabinet, cloud storage online, or electronic storage devices in multiple physical locations. Update every six months or when major life events occur.

Emergency Items and Contacts:

Keep updated mailing addresses, email, and phone numbers for emergency contacts (e.g., executors, investment or financial professionals, attorneys, insurance agents, accountants, CPAs, tax preparers, supervisors, medical professionals to include dentist and doctors, home health aides, family members, and more).

Documents required upon serious injury or death include:

- ♦ Copy of health care proxy (living will)
- ♦ Durable power of attorney (financial and medical)

- Financial institutions' power of attorney forms completed (may be proprietary)
- Certified copy of last will and testament
- Trust
- Instruction letter for the executor
- Donation preference to family, friends, and charities
- Location of safe with access (keys or combination)
- Safety deposit box keys
- List of online accounts and passwords
- Burial instructions—funeral home and burial plot deed
- Birth certificate (death certificate for the deceased)
- Obituary information (resume or bio)
- Discharge papers for military
- Passport/citizenship (naturalization papers)
- Phone number and address of County Surrogate for Orphans or Orphan's Court (to probate a will)

Documents for Financial and Health Insurance and Other Items

- Investment and assets management
- Banks, credit unions, fintech, mortgages, and loans
- Mutual funds and equities
- Retirement and pension plans
- Other corporate benefits
- Health insurance
- Life insurance and long-term care insurance
- Property and casualty insurance
- Annuities to include social security
- Trusts and other financial plans
- Tax documents
- Titles and deeds
- Credit cards

- Other legal documents
- Telephone and cell phones
- Utilities
- Warranties, service contracts, and instructions

Emergency Information:
Ready Accessible Documents

- Social Security Card
- Birth Certificate
- Passport or Naturalization Papers
- Driver's License (# with expiration date)
- Marriage Certificate
- Divorce or Separation Papers
- Prenuptial Agreements
- Adoption Papers
- Safe and Safe Deposit Box Keys and/or Combinations

Broad Categories of Emergency Papers/ Information:
Emergency Documents to Settle Claims

- Investment Documents (transfer ownership)
    - Per Credit Applications
    - Per Last Will and Testament
- Insurance and Annuity Documents (to settle claims)
- Bank and Credit Documents
    - Access to Cash to Settle Estate Affairs
    - Documents to Settle Outstanding Credit Accounts
- Personal Finance Documents
    - Transfer Ownership Per Last Will and Testament
    - Documents Needed to Settle Debts
- Items for the Seriously Ill
    - Living Will and Health Care Proxy

- ○ Durable Power of Attorney (POA)
- ○ Financial Institution's Proprietary POA
- ♦ Items for the Recently Deceased

Items for the recently deceased are the following:

- ♦ Last will and testament
- ♦ Military discharge papers, if applicable
- ♦ Burial instructions
- ♦ Cemetery plot deed, prepaid cremation documents
- ♦ Funeral home preference and information
- ♦ Charitable donations, if applicable
- ♦ A letter of instruction
- ♦ Death certificate (order at least 10)
- ♦ Information for the obituary
- ♦ The phone number of your County Surrogate Court (i.e., the county clerk or clerk's office to probate the last will and testament by the executor)

The executor should obtain enough death certificates to transfer the ownership of all accounts and titles of ownership for the deceased.

AUTHOR BIO

Portrait by daughter
Ms. Madison A. Moore

As seen on Dayton NBC and CBS news affiliates, Spectrum News 1, Fox Soul TV's Black Agenda Report, Black New Channel, and more, Edmund H. Moore PhD is active in the community. He is a senior engineer and program manager at Wright-Patterson Air Force Base in Ohio.

Dr. Moore has the privilege of chairing the 2022 Dayton District's Combined Federal Campaign. Currently, he is a co-chair of Parity Inc. He serves on the Phoenix Next Board, the Advisory Board for the Virginia Tech Materials Science & Engineering Department, and is on the Finance Committee for The Dayton Foundation. Edmund is a past board member of the CityWide Development Corporation and a past board member of a start-up and real estate investment partner.

Edmund is a member of Sigma Pi Phi Fraternity, the Omega Psi Phi Fraternity, Inc., the Omega Baptist Church, the National Society of Black Engineers, Sigma Xi, the American Ceramic Society (ACerS), the Air Force Association, and the Keramos Fraternity.

Dr. Moore is the recipient of several awards, including a Secretary of the Air Force (SAF) Special Achievement Award, an Air Force Award for Meritorious Civilian Service, a Black Engineer of the Year Award, the Florida A&M University National Alumni Association (NAA) Distinguished Alumni Award—In Field of Technology, a Wright-Patterson AFB 2015 Diversity Leadership Awards, and numerous others.

Edmund is the proud father of two daughters, Mackenzie and Madison. He authored the acclaimed *With a Father's Love: 52 Weekly Letters to My Beloved Daughters* sold at Amazon.com and a book for Parity Inc. titled *Village Wisdom for Our Youth*, with Lift Bridge Publishing. All proceeds go to Parity Inc.

Both books are available for purchase at Amazon.com

Lightning Source UK Ltd.
Milton Keynes UK
UKHW020808041122
411637UK00015B/616

9 798885 675789